THIS BOOK BELONGS TO:

MY BIKES

Model: _____

Type: ☐ ☐ ☐ ☐ ☐

Frame No.: _____

Color: _____

Characteristics: _____

Model: _____

Type: ☐ ☐ ☐ ☐ ☐

Frame No.: _____

Color: _____

Characteristics: _____

Model: _____

Type: ☐ ☐ ☐ ☐ ☐

Frame No.: _____

Color: _____

Characteristics: _____

MY BIKES

Model: _____

Type: ☐ ☐ ☐ ☐ ☐

Frame No.: _____

Color: _____

Characteristics: _____

Model: _____

Type: ☐ ☐ ☐ ☐ ☐

Frame No.: _____

Color: _____

Characteristics: _____

Model: _____

Type: ☐ ☐ ☐ ☐ ☐

Frame No.: _____

Color: _____

Characteristics: _____

MY TOUR LOG

Name

Date

Time

Total Time

Distance

Bike

Riders along

Location

Bike Park ☐   Trail Park ☐   Cross Country ☐

Ø Speed   Top Speed

Elevation Gain

Difficulty ① ② ③ ④ ⑤   Fitness level ① ② ③ ④ ⑤

Fun factor ① ② ③ ④ ⑤   Ride again? ① ② ③ ④ ⑤

Weather ☀ ⛅ 🌤 🌧 🌨   Temperature

QUOTE OF THE DAY

What the hell of a tour   ⑤

MY TOUR LOG

Name

Date	Location
Time	Bike Park ☐ Trail Park ☐ Cross Country ☐
Total Time	Ø Speed Top Speed
Distance	Elevation Gain
Bike	
Riders along	

Difficulty	① ② ③ ④ ⑤	Fitness level	① ② ③ ④ ⑤
Fun factor	① ② ③ ④ ⑤	Ride again?	① ② ③ ④ ⑤

Weather   Temperature

QUOTE OF THE DAY

What the hell of a tour   ① ② ③ ④ ⑤

MY TOUR LOG

Name

Date	Location
Time	Bike Park ☐ Trail Park ☐ Cross Country ☐
Total Time	Ø Speed Top Speed
Distance	Elevation Gain
Bike	
Riders along	

Difficulty ① ② ③ ④ ⑤   Fitness level ① ② ③ ④ ⑤

Fun factor ① ② ③ ④ ⑤   Ride again? ① ② ③ ④ ⑤

Weather ☀ ⛅ 🌤 🌧 🌨   Temperature

QUOTE OF THE DAY

What the hell of a tour

MY TOUR LOG

Name

Date	Location
Time	Bike Park ☐ Trail Park ☐ Cross Country ☐
Total Time	Ø Speed Top Speed
Distance	Elevation Gain
Bike	
Riders along	

Difficulty ① ② ③ ④ ⑤   Fitness level ① ② ③ ④ ⑤

Fun factor ① ② ③ ④ ⑤   Ride again? ① ② ③ ④ ⑤

Weather ☀ ☁ ⛅ 🌧 🌨   Temperature

QUOTE OF THE DAY

What the hell of a tour ① ② ③ ④ ⑤

MY TOUR LOG

Name

Date

Time

Total Time

Distance

Bike

Riders along

Location

Bike Park ☐ Trail Park ☐ Cross Country ☐

Ø Speed   Top Speed

Elevation Gain

Difficulty	① ② ③ ④ ⑤	Fitness level	① ② ③ ④ ⑤
Fun factor	① ② ③ ④ ⑤	Ride again?	① ② ③ ④ ⑤

Weather ☀ ☁ 🌦 🌧 🌨   Temperature

QUOTE OF THE DAY

. . . .
. . . .
. . . .
. . . .

What the hell of a tour   ① ② ③ ④ ⑤

MY TOUR LOG

Name

Date	Location
Time	Bike Park ☐ Trail Park ☐ Cross Country ☐
Total Time	Ø Speed Top Speed
Distance	Elevation Gain

Bike

Riders along

Difficulty   ① ② ③ ④ ⑤   Fitness level   ① ② ③ ④ ⑤

Fun factor   ① ② ③ ④ ⑤   Ride again?   ① ② ③ ④ ⑤

Weather   ☀   ☁   ⛅   🌧   🌨   Temperature

QUOTE OF THE DAY

What the hell of a tour   ① ② ③ ④ ⑤

MY TOUR LOG

Name

Date	
Time	

Location	
Bike Park ☐ Trail Park ☐ Cross Country ☐

Total Time	
Ø Speed	Top Speed

Distance	
Elevation Gain	

Bike

Riders along

Difficulty	①	②	③	④	⑤	Fitness level	①	②	③	④	⑤
Fun factor	①	②	③	④	⑤	Ride again?	①	②	③	④	⑤

Weather ☀ ☁ 🌤 🌧 🌨   Temperature

QUOTE OF THE DAY

. . . .
. . . .
. . . .

What the hell of a tour

MY TOUR LOG

Name

Date		Location
Time		Bike Park ☐ Trail Park ☐ Cross Country ☐
Total Time		Ø Speed Top Speed
Distance		Elevation Gain
Bike		
Riders along		

Difficulty   ① ② ③ ④ ⑤   Fitness level   ① ② ③ ④ ⑤

Fun factor   ① ② ③ ④ ⑤   Ride again?   ① ② ③ ④ ⑤

Weather   ☀   ☁   ⛅   🌧   🌨   Temperature

QUOTE OF THE DAY

What the hell of a tour   ④   ⑤

MY TOUR LOG

Name

Date

Location

Time

Bike Park ☐   Trail Park ☐   Cross Country ☐

Total Time

Ø Speed   Top Speed

Distance

Elevation Gain

Bike

Riders along

Difficulty   ① ② ③ ④ ⑤   Fitness level   ① ② ③ ④ ⑤

Fun factor   ① ② ③ ④ ⑤   Ride again?   ① ② ③ ④ ⑤

Weather ☀ ☁ ⛅ 🌧 🌨   Temperature

QUOTE OF THE DAY

What the hell of a tour   ①   ②   ③   ④   ⑤

MY TOUR LOG

Name

Date	Location
Time	Bike Park ☐ Trail Park ☐ Cross Country ☐
Total Time	Ø Speed Top Speed
Distance	Elevation Gain
Bike	
Riders along	

Difficulty ① ② ③ ④ ⑤   Fitness level ① ② ③ ④ ⑤

Fun factor ① ② ③ ④ ⑤   Ride again? ① ② ③ ④ ⑤

Weather ☀ ☁ ⛅ 🌧 🌨   Temperature

QUOTE OF THE DAY

What the hell of a tour ① ② ③ ④ ⑤

MY TOUR LOG

Name

Date		Location	
Time		Bike Park ☐ Trail Park ☐ Cross Country ☐
Total Time		Ø Speed		Top Speed	
Distance		Elevation Gain	
Bike	
Riders along	

Difficulty ① ② ③ ④ ⑤   Fitness level ① ② ③ ④ ⑤

Fun factor ① ② ③ ④ ⑤   Ride again?   ① ② ③ ④ ⑤

Weather ☀ ☁ ⛅ 🌧 🌨   Temperature [   ]

QUOTE OF THE DAY

What the hell of a tour

MY TOUR LOG

Name

Date | Location

Time | Bike Park ☐ Trail Park ☐ Cross Country ☐

Total Time | Ø Speed | Top Speed

Distance | Elevation Gain

Bike

Riders along

Difficulty ① ② ③ ④ ⑤   Fitness level ① ② ③ ④ ⑤

Fun factor ① ② ③ ④ ⑤   Ride again? ① ② ③ ④ ⑤

Weather   ☀   ☁   ⛅   🌧   🌨   Temperature

QUOTE OF THE DAY

What the hell of a tour   ①   ②   ③   ④   ⑤

MY TOUR LOG

Name

Date		Location
Time		Bike Park ☐ Trail Park ☐ Cross Country ☐
Total Time		Ø Speed	Top Speed
Distance		Elevation Gain
Bike		
Riders along		

Difficulty ① ② ③ ④ ⑤   Fitness level ① ② ③ ④ ⑤

Fun factor ① ② ③ ④ ⑤   Ride again? ① ② ③ ④ ⑤

Weather ☀ ☁ ⛅ 🌧 🌨   Temperature

QUOTE OF THE DAY

What the hell of a tour

MY TOUR LOG

Name

Date | Location

Time | Bike Park ☐ Trail Park ☐ Cross Country ☐

Total Time | Ø Speed | Top Speed

Distance | Elevation Gain

Bike

Riders along

Difficulty ① ② ③ ④ ⑤   Fitness level ① ② ③ ④ ⑤

Fun factor ① ② ③ ④ ⑤   Ride again? ① ② ③ ④ ⑤

Weather ☀ ☁ 🌤 🌧 🌨   Temperature

QUOTE OF THE DAY

What the hell of a tour ① ② ③ ④ ⑤

MY TOUR LOG

Name

Date

Time

Total Time   Ø Speed   Top Speed

Distance   Elevation Gain

Bike

Riders along

Location

Bike Park ☐   Trail Park ☐   Cross Country ☐

Difficulty   ① ② ③ ④ ⑤   Fitness level   ① ② ③ ④ ⑤

Fun factor   ① ② ③ ④ ⑤   Ride again?   ① ② ③ ④ ⑤

Weather   ☀ ☁ ⛅ 🌧 🌨   Temperature

QUOTE OF THE DAY

What the hell of a tour

MY TOUR LOG

Name

Date	Location
Time	Bike Park ☐ Trail Park ☐ Cross Country ☐
Total Time	Ø Speed Top Speed
Distance	Elevation Gain
Bike	
Riders along	

Difficulty   ① ② ③ ④ ⑤   Fitness level   ① ② ③ ④ ⑤

Fun factor   ① ② ③ ④ ⑤   Ride again?   ① ② ③ ④ ⑤

Weather   🔆 ☁️ 🌦️ 🌧️ 🌨️   Temperature

QUOTE OF THE DAY

What the hell of a tour

MY TOUR LOG

Name

Date   Location

Time   Bike Park ☐   Trail Park ☐   Cross Country ☐

Total Time   Ø Speed   Top Speed

Distance   Elevation Gain

Bike

Riders along

Difficulty	① ② ③ ④ ⑤		Fitness level	① ② ③ ④ ⑤
Fun factor	① ② ③ ④ ⑤		Ride again?	① ② ③ ④ ⑤

Weather ☀ ⛅ 🌦 🌧 🌨   Temperature

QUOTE OF THE DAY

What the hell of a tour

MY TOUR LOG

Name

Date	Location
Time	Bike Park ☐ Trail Park ☐ Cross Country ☐
Total Time	Ø Speed Top Speed
Distance	Elevation Gain
Bike	
Riders along	

Difficulty ① ② ③ ④ ⑤   Fitness level ① ② ③ ④ ⑤

Fun factor ① ② ③ ④ ⑤   Ride again? ① ② ③ ④ ⑤

Weather ☀ ☁ ⛅ 🌧 🌨   Temperature

QUOTE OF THE DAY

What the hell of a tour ① ② ③ ④ ⑤

MY TOUR LOG

Name

Date

Time

Total Time

Distance

Bike

Riders along

Location	
Bike Park ☐	Trail Park ☐	Cross Country ☐
Ø Speed	Top Speed
Elevation Gain	

Difficulty ① ② ③ ④ ⑤   Fitness level ① ② ③ ④ ⑤

Fun factor ① ② ③ ④ ⑤   Ride again? ① ② ③ ④ ⑤

Weather ☀ ☁ ⛅ 🌧 🌨   Temperature

QUOTE OF THE DAY

What the hell of a tour

MY TOUR LOG

Name

Date	
Time	

Location

Bike Park ☐ Trail Park ☐ Cross Country ☐

Total Time		Ø Speed	Top Speed
Distance		Elevation Gain	

Bike

Riders along

Difficulty	① ② ③ ④ ⑤
Fun factor	① ② ③ ④ ⑤

Fitness level	① ② ③ ④ ⑤
Ride again?	① ② ③ ④ ⑤

Weather ☀ ☁ 🌤 🌧 🌨   Temperature

QUOTE OF THE DAY

What the hell of a tour   ① ② ③ ④ ⑤

MY TOUR LOG

Name

Date	Location
Time	Bike Park ☐ Trail Park ☐ Cross Country ☐
Total Time	Ø Speed Top Speed
Distance	Elevation Gain
Bike	
Riders along	

Difficulty ① ② ③ ④ ⑤   Fitness level ① ② ③ ④ ⑤

Fun factor ① ② ③ ④ ⑤   Ride again?   ① ② ③ ④ ⑤

Weather ☀ ☁ ⛅ 🌧 🌨   Temperature

QUOTE OF THE DAY

What the hell of a tour

MY TOUR LOG

Name

Date

Location

Time

Bike Park ☐   Trail Park ☐   Cross Country ☐

Total Time

Ø Speed

Top Speed

Distance

Elevation Gain

Bike

Riders along

Difficulty	① ② ③ ④ ⑤	Fitness level	① ② ③ ④ ⑤
Fun factor	① ② ③ ④ ⑤	Ride again?	① ② ③ ④ ⑤

Weather ☀ ☁ 🌤 🌧 🌨   Temperature

QUOTE OF THE DAY

What the hell of a tour   ①   ②   ③   ④   ⑤

MY TOUR LOG

Name

Date		Location	
Time		Bike Park ☐ Trail Park ☐ Cross Country ☐
Total Time		Ø Speed	Top Speed
Distance		Elevation Gain	
Bike			
Riders along			

Difficulty	① ② ③ ④ ⑤	Fitness level	① ② ③ ④ ⑤
Fun factor	① ② ③ ④ ⑤	Ride again?	① ② ③ ④ ⑤

Weather ☀ ☁ ⛅ 🌧 🌨   Temperature

QUOTE OF THE DAY

What the hell of a tour   ① ② ③ ④ ⑤

MY TOUR LOG

Name

Date

Location

Time

Bike Park ☐ Trail Park ☐ Cross Country ☐

Total Time

Ø Speed

Top Speed

Distance

Elevation Gain

Bike

Riders along

Difficulty	① ② ③ ④ ⑤	Fitness level	① ② ③ ④ ⑤
Fun factor	① ② ③ ④ ⑤	Ride again?	① ② ③ ④ ⑤

Weather ☀ ☁ ⛅ 🌧 🌨 Temperature

QUOTE OF THE DAY

What the hell of a tour ① ② ③ ④ ⑤

MY TOUR LOG

Name

Date

Location

Time

Bike Park ☐ Trail Park ☐ Cross Country ☐

Total Time

Ø Speed

Top Speed

Distance

Elevation Gain

Bike

Riders along

Difficulty   ① ② ③ ④ ⑤   Fitness level   ① ② ③ ④ ⑤

Fun factor   ① ② ③ ④ ⑤   Ride again?   ① ② ③ ④ ⑤

Weather ☀ ⛅ 🌤 🌧 🌨   Temperature

QUOTE OF THE DAY

What the hell of a tour   ⑤

MY TOUR LOG

Name

Date	Location
Time	Bike Park ☐ Trail Park ☐ Cross Country ☐
Total Time	Ø Speed Top Speed
Distance	Elevation Gain
Bike	
Riders along	

Difficulty ① ② ③ ④ ⑤   Fitness level ① ② ③ ④ ⑤

Fun factor ① ② ③ ④ ⑤   Ride again? ① ② ③ ④ ⑤

Weather ☀ ☁ ⛅ 🌧 🌨   Temperature

QUOTE OF THE DAY

What the hell of a tour ① ② ③ ④ ⑤

MY TOUR LOG

Name

Date		Location	
Time		Bike Park ☐ Trail Park ☐ Cross Country ☐
Total Time		Ø Speed	Top Speed
Distance		Elevation Gain	
Bike			
Riders along			

Difficulty　① ② ③ ④ ⑤　　Fitness level　① ② ③ ④ ⑤

Fun factor　① ② ③ ④ ⑤　　Ride again?　① ② ③ ④ ⑤

Weather ☀ ⛅ 🌦 🌧 🌨　Temperature [ ]

QUOTE OF THE DAY

What the hell of a tour

MY TOUR LOG

Name

Date

Location

Time

Bike Park ☐　Trail Park ☐　Cross Country ☐

Total Time

Ø Speed　　　Top Speed

Distance

Elevation Gain

Bike

Riders along

Difficulty	① ② ③ ④ ⑤	Fitness level	① ② ③ ④ ⑤
Fun factor	① ② ③ ④ ⑤	Ride again?	① ② ③ ④ ⑤

Weather ☀ ☁ ⛅ 🌧 🌨　Temperature

QUOTE OF THE DAY

What the hell of a tour　① ② ③ ④ ⑤

MY TOUR LOG

Name

Date | Location

Time | Bike Park ☐ Trail Park ☐ Cross Country ☐

Total Time | Ø Speed | Top Speed

Distance | Elevation Gain

Bike

Riders along

Difficulty ① ② ③ ④ ⑤   Fitness level ① ② ③ ④ ⑤

Fun factor ① ② ③ ④ ⑤   Ride again? ① ② ③ ④ ⑤

Weather ☀ ☁ 🌤 🌧 🌨   Temperature

QUOTE OF THE DAY

What the hell of a tour

MY TOUR LOG

Name

Date | Location

Time | Bike Park ☐ Trail Park ☐ Cross Country ☐

Total Time | Ø Speed | Top Speed

Distance | Elevation Gain

Bike

Riders along

Difficulty ① ② ③ ④ ⑤ | Fitness level ① ② ③ ④ ⑤

Fun factor ① ② ③ ④ ⑤ | Ride again? ① ② ③ ④ ⑤

Weather ☀ ☁ ⛅ 🌧 🌨 | Temperature

QUOTE OF THE DAY

What the hell of a tour ① ② ③ ④ ⑤

MY TOUR LOG

Name

Date	
Time	
Total Time	
Distance	
Bike	
Riders along	

Location	
Bike Park ☐ Trail Park ☐ Cross Country ☐	
Ø Speed	Top Speed
Elevation Gain	

Difficulty ① ② ③ ④ ⑤   Fitness level ① ② ③ ④ ⑤

Fun factor ① ② ③ ④ ⑤   Ride again? ① ② ③ ④ ⑤

Weather   Temperature

QUOTE OF THE DAY

What the hell of a tour

MY TOUR LOG

Name

Date	Location
Time	Bike Park ☐ Trail Park ☐ Cross Country ☐
Total Time	Ø Speed Top Speed
Distance	Elevation Gain
Bike	
Riders along	

Difficulty ① ② ③ ④ ⑤   Fitness level ① ② ③ ④ ⑤

Fun factor ① ② ③ ④ ⑤   Ride again? ① ② ③ ④ ⑤

Weather ☀ ⛅ 🌤 🌧 🌨   Temperature

QUOTE OF THE DAY

What the hell of a tour   ① ② ③ ④ ⑤

MY TOUR LOG

Name

Date		Location	
Time		Bike Park ☐ Trail Park ☐ Cross Country ☐
Total Time		Ø Speed	Top Speed
Distance		Elevation Gain	
Bike			
Riders along			

Difficulty ① ② ③ ④ ⑤   Fitness level ① ② ③ ④ ⑤

Fun factor ① ② ③ ④ ⑤   Ride again? ① ② ③ ④ ⑤

Weather ☀ ⛅ 🌦 🌧 🌨   Temperature

QUOTE OF THE DAY

What the hell of a tour

MY TOUR LOG

Name

Date		Location
Time		Bike Park ☐ Trail Park ☐ Cross Country ☐
Total Time		Ø Speed __ Top Speed __
Distance		Elevation Gain
Bike		
Riders along		

Difficulty ① ② ③ ④ ⑤   Fitness level ① ② ③ ④ ⑤

Fun factor ① ② ③ ④ ⑤   Ride again? ① ② ③ ④ ⑤

Weather ☀ ☁ ⛅ 🌦 🌨   Temperature __

QUOTE OF THE DAY

What the hell of a tour   ①   ②   ③   ④   ⑤

MY TOUR LOG

Name

Date

Location

Time

Bike Park ☐   Trail Park ☐   Cross Country ☐

Total Time

Ø Speed   Top Speed

Distance

Elevation Gain

Bike

Riders along

| Difficulty | ① ② ③ ④ ⑤ | Fitness level | ① ② ③ ④ ⑤ |
| Fun factor | ① ② ③ ④ ⑤ | Ride again? | ① ② ③ ④ ⑤ |

Weather   ☀   ☁   ⛅   🌧   ❄   Temperature

QUOTE OF THE DAY

What the hell of a tour

MY TOUR LOG

Name

Date	Location
Time	Bike Park ☐ Trail Park ☐ Cross Country ☐
Total Time	Ø Speed Top Speed
Distance	Elevation Gain
Bike	
Riders along	

Difficulty ① ② ③ ④ ⑤   Fitness level ① ② ③ ④ ⑤

Fun factor ① ② ③ ④ ⑤   Ride again? ① ② ③ ④ ⑤

Weather ☀ ⛅ 🌦 🌧 🌨   Temperature

QUOTE OF THE DAY

What the hell of a tour   ④ ⑤

MY TOUR LOG

Name

Date	Location
Time	Bike Park ☐ Trail Park ☐ Cross Country ☐
Total Time	Ø Speed Top Speed
Distance	Elevation Gain

Bike

Riders along

Difficulty	① ② ③ ④ ⑤
Fun factor	① ② ③ ④ ⑤

Fitness level	① ② ③ ④ ⑤
Ride again?	① ② ③ ④ ⑤

Weather ☀ ☁ ⛅ 🌧 🌨   Temperature

QUOTE OF THE DAY

What the hell of a tour

MY TOUR LOG

Name

Date	
Time	Location
	Bike Park ☐ Trail Park ☐ Cross Country ☐
Total Time	Ø Speed Top Speed
Distance	Elevation Gain
Bike	
Riders along	

Difficulty ① ② ③ ④ ⑤   Fitness level ① ② ③ ④ ⑤

Fun factor ① ② ③ ④ ⑤   Ride again? ① ② ③ ④ ⑤

Weather ☀ ⛅ 🌤 🌧 🌨   Temperature

QUOTE OF THE DAY

What the hell of a tour   ① ② ③ ④ ⑤

MY TOUR LOG

Name

Date		Location
Time		Bike Park ☐ Trail Park ☐ Cross Country ☐
Total Time		Ø Speed Top Speed
Distance		Elevation Gain
Bike		
Riders along		

Difficulty	① ② ③ ④ ⑤	Fitness level	① ② ③ ④ ⑤
Fun factor	① ② ③ ④ ⑤	Ride again?	① ② ③ ④ ⑤

Weather   Temperature

QUOTE OF THE DAY

What the hell of a tour   ①   ②   ③   ④   ⑤

MY TOUR LOG

Name

Date		Location
Time		Bike Park ☐ Trail Park ☐ Cross Country ☐
Total Time		Ø Speed	Top Speed
Distance		Elevation Gain

Bike

Riders along

Difficulty ① ② ③ ④ ⑤   Fitness level ① ② ③ ④ ⑤

Fun factor ① ② ③ ④ ⑤   Ride again? ① ② ③ ④ ⑤

Weather ☀ ☁ 🌦 🌧 🌨   Temperature

QUOTE OF THE DAY

What the hell of a tour ① ② ③ ④ ⑤

MY TOUR LOG

Name

Date

Time

Total Time

Distance

Bike

Riders along

Location

Bike Park ☐   Trail Park ☐   Cross Country ☐

Ø Speed   Top Speed

Elevation Gain

Difficulty   ① ② ③ ④ ⑤   Fitness level   ① ② ③ ④ ⑤

Fun factor   ① ② ③ ④ ⑤   Ride again?   ① ② ③ ④ ⑤

Weather   Temperature

QUOTE OF THE DAY

What the hell of a tour

MY TOUR LOG

Name

Date	Location
Time	Bike Park ☐ Trail Park ☐ Cross Country ☐
Total Time	Ø Speed Top Speed
Distance	Elevation Gain
Bike	
Riders along	

Difficulty ① ② ③ ④ ⑤   Fitness level ① ② ③ ④ ⑤

Fun factor ① ② ③ ④ ⑤   Ride again? ① ② ③ ④ ⑤

Weather ☀ ☁ 🌤 🌧 🌨   Temperature

QUOTE OF THE DAY

What the hell of a tour   ④ ⑤

MY TOUR LOG

Name

Date

Time

Total Time   Ø Speed   Top Speed

Distance   Elevation Gain

Bike

Riders along

Location

Bike Park ☐   Trail Park ☐   Cross Country ☐

Difficulty   ① ② ③ ④ ⑤   Fitness level   ① ② ③ ④ ⑤

Fun factor   ① ② ③ ④ ⑤   Ride again?   ① ② ③ ④ ⑤

Weather   Temperature

QUOTE OF THE DAY

What the hell of a tour

MY TOUR LOG

Name

Date		Location	

Time

Bike Park ☐   Trail Park ☐   Cross Country ☐

Total Time		Ø Speed		Top Speed	

Distance		Elevation Gain	

Bike

Riders along

Difficulty	① ② ③ ④ ⑤	Fitness level	① ② ③ ④ ⑤
Fun factor	① ② ③ ④ ⑤	Ride again?	① ② ③ ④ ⑤

Weather ☀ ☁ 🌦 🌧 🌨   Temperature

QUOTE OF THE DAY

What the hell of a tour   ③ ⑤

MY TOUR LOG

Name

Date	
Time	Location
	Bike Park ☐ Trail Park ☐ Cross Country ☐
Total Time	Ø Speed Top Speed
Distance	Elevation Gain
Bike	
Riders along	

Difficulty ① ② ③ ④ ⑤   Fitness level ① ② ③ ④ ⑤

Fun factor ① ② ③ ④ ⑤   Ride again? ① ② ③ ④ ⑤

Weather ☀ ☁ ⛅ 🌧 🌨   Temperature

QUOTE OF THE DAY

What the hell of a tour ① ② ③ ④ ⑤

MY TOUR LOG

Name

Date

Location

Time

Bike Park ☐   Trail Park ☐   Cross Country ☐

Total Time

Ø Speed

Top Speed

Distance

Elevation Gain

Bike

Riders along

Difficulty   ① ② ③ ④ ⑤   Fitness level   ① ② ③ ④ ⑤

Fun factor   ① ② ③ ④ ⑤   Ride again?   ① ② ③ ④ ⑤

Weather ☀ ☁ 🌦 🌧 🌨   Temperature

QUOTE OF THE DAY

What the hell of a tour   ③ ④

MY TOUR LOG

Name

Date

Time

Total Time

Distance

Bike

Riders along

Location

Bike Park ☐   Trail Park ☐   Cross Country ☐

Ø Speed   Top Speed

Elevation Gain

Difficulty	① ② ③ ④ ⑤	Fitness level	① ② ③ ④ ⑤
Fun factor	① ② ③ ④ ⑤	Ride again?	① ② ③ ④ ⑤

Weather   Temperature

QUOTE OF THE DAY

What the hell of a tour   ① ② ③ ④ ⑤

MY TOUR LOG

Name

Date

Location

Time

Bike Park ☐   Trail Park ☐   Cross Country ☐

Total Time

Ø Speed

Top Speed

Distance

Elevation Gain

Bike

Riders along

Difficulty	① ② ③ ④ ⑤	Fitness level	① ② ③ ④ ⑤
Fun factor	① ② ③ ④ ⑤	Ride again?	① ② ③ ④ ⑤

Weather   ☀   ⛅   🌦   🌧   🌨   Temperature

QUOTE OF THE DAY

What the hell of a tour   ①   ②   ③   ④   ⑤

MY TOUR LOG

Name

Date

Location

Time

Bike Park ☐   Trail Park ☐   Cross Country ☐

Total Time

Ø Speed   Top Speed

Distance

Elevation Gain

Bike

Riders along

Difficulty   ① ② ③ ④ ⑤   Fitness level   ① ② ③ ④ ⑤

Fun factor   ① ② ③ ④ ⑤   Ride again?   ① ② ③ ④ ⑤

Weather   ☀ ⛅ 🌤 🌧 🌨   Temperature

QUOTE OF THE DAY

What the hell of a tour   ① ② ③ ④ ⑤

MY TOUR LOG

Name

Date	Location
Time	Bike Park ☐ Trail Park ☐ Cross Country ☐
Total Time	Ø Speed Top Speed
Distance	Elevation Gain

Bike

Riders along

Difficulty	①	②	③	④	⑤	Fitness level	①	②	③	④	⑤
Fun factor	①	②	③	④	⑤	Ride again?	①	②	③	④	⑤

Weather ☀ ☁ ⛅ 🌧 🌨   Temperature

QUOTE OF THE DAY

What the hell of a tour

MY TOUR LOG

Name

Date

Time

Total Time   Ø Speed   Top Speed

Distance   Elevation Gain

Bike

Riders along

Difficulty   ① ② ③ ④ ⑤   Fitness level   ① ② ③ ④ ⑤

Fun factor   ① ② ③ ④ ⑤   Ride again?   ① ② ③ ④ ⑤

Location

Bike Park ☐   Trail Park ☐   Cross Country ☐

Weather   Temperature

QUOTE OF THE DAY

What the hell of a tour

MY TOUR LOG

Name

Date

Location

Time

Bike Park ☐   Trail Park ☐   Cross Country ☐

Total Time

Ø Speed

Top Speed

Distance

Elevation Gain

Bike

Riders along

| Difficulty | ① ② ③ ④ ⑤ | Fitness level | ① ② ③ ④ ⑤ |
| Fun factor | ① ② ③ ④ ⑤ | Ride again? | ① ② ③ ④ ⑤ |

Weather ☀ ☁ 🌤 🌧 🌨   Temperature

QUOTE OF THE DAY

What the hell of a tour   ①   ②   ③   ④   ⑤

MY TOUR LOG

Name

Date | Location

Time | Bike Park ☐ Trail Park ☐ Cross Country ☐

Total Time | Ø Speed | Top Speed

Distance | Elevation Gain

Bike

Riders along

| Difficulty | ① ② ③ ④ ⑤ | Fitness level | ① ② ③ ④ ⑤ |
| Fun factor | ① ② ③ ④ ⑤ | Ride again? | ① ② ③ ④ ⑤ |

Weather ☀ ☁ ⛅ 🌧 🌨   Temperature

QUOTE OF THE DAY

What the hell of a tour   ① ② ③ ④ ⑤

MY TOUR LOG

Name

Date		Location
Time		Bike Park ☐ Trail Park ☐ Cross Country ☐
Total Time		Ø Speed [ ] Top Speed [ ]
Distance		Elevation Gain
Bike		
Riders along		

Difficulty ① ② ③ ④ ⑤   Fitness level ① ② ③ ④ ⑤

Fun factor ① ② ③ ④ ⑤   Ride again? ① ② ③ ④ ⑤

Weather ☼ ☁ ⛅ 🌧 🌨   Temperature [ ]

QUOTE OF THE DAY

What the hell of a tour   ①   ②   ③   ④   ⑤

MY TOUR LOG

Name

Date

Location

Time

Bike Park ☐   Trail Park ☐   Cross Country ☐

Total Time

Ø Speed

Top Speed

Distance

Elevation Gain

Bike

Riders along

Difficulty	① ② ③ ④ ⑤	Fitness level	① ② ③ ④ ⑤
Fun factor	① ② ③ ④ ⑤	Ride again?	① ② ③ ④ ⑤

Weather   ☀   ☁   🌤   🌧   🌨   Temperature

QUOTE OF THE DAY

What the hell of a tour   ①   ②   ③   ④   ⑤

MY TOUR LOG

Name

Date

Location

Time

Bike Park ☐ Trail Park ☐ Cross Country ☐

Total Time

Ø Speed

Top Speed

Distance

Elevation Gain

Bike

Riders along

Difficulty   ① ② ③ ④ ⑤   Fitness level   ① ② ③ ④ ⑤

Fun factor   ① ② ③ ④ ⑤   Ride again?   ① ② ③ ④ ⑤

Weather   ☀ ☁ 🌤 🌧 🌨   Temperature

QUOTE OF THE DAY

What the hell of a tour   ① ② ③ ④ ⑤

MY TOUR LOG

Name

Date

Location

Time

Bike Park ☐   Trail Park ☐   Cross Country ☐

Total Time

Ø Speed   Top Speed

Distance

Elevation Gain

Bike

Riders along

Difficulty   ① ② ③ ④ ⑤   Fitness level   ① ② ③ ④ ⑤

Fun factor   ① ② ③ ④ ⑤   Ride again?   ① ② ③ ④ ⑤

Weather   ☀ ☁ 🌦 🌧 🌨   Temperature

QUOTE OF THE DAY

What the hell of a tour

MY TOUR LOG

Name

Date

Time

Bike Park ☐   Trail Park ☐   Cross Country ☐

Location

Total Time   Ø Speed   Top Speed

Distance   Elevation Gain

Bike

Riders along

| Difficulty | ① ② ③ ④ ⑤ | Fitness level | ① ② ③ ④ ⑤ |
| Fun factor | ① ② ③ ④ ⑤ | Ride again? | ① ② ③ ④ ⑤ |

Weather   ☀   ☁   🌦   🌧   🌨   Temperature

QUOTE OF THE DAY

What the hell of a tour   ①   ②   ③   ④   ⑤

MY TOUR LOG

Name

Date		Location	
Time		Bike Park ☐	Trail Park ☐ Cross Country ☐
Total Time		Ø Speed	Top Speed
Distance		Elevation Gain	

Bike

Riders along

Difficulty	① ② ③ ④ ⑤
Fun factor	① ② ③ ④ ⑤

Fitness level	① ② ③ ④ ⑤
Ride again?	① ② ③ ④ ⑤

Weather ☀ ☁ 🌦 🌧 🌨   Temperature

QUOTE OF THE DAY

What the hell of a tour ② ③ ④ ⑤

MY TOUR LOG

Name

Date

Location

Time

Bike Park ☐   Trail Park ☐   Cross Country ☐

Total Time

Ø Speed

Top Speed

Distance

Elevation Gain

Bike

Riders along

Difficulty   ① ② ③ ④ ⑤

Fitness level   ① ② ③ ④ ⑤

Fun factor   ① ② ③ ④ ⑤

Ride again?   ① ② ③ ④ ⑤

Weather   ☀   ☁   🌤   🌧   🌨   Temperature

QUOTE OF THE DAY

What the hell of a tour   ① ② ③ ④ ⑤

MY TOUR LOG

Name

Date	Location
Time	Bike Park ☐ Trail Park ☐ Cross Country ☐
Total Time	Ø Speed Top Speed
Distance	Elevation Gain
Bike	
Riders along	

Difficulty ① ② ③ ④ ⑤   Fitness level ① ② ③ ④ ⑤

Fun factor ① ② ③ ④ ⑤   Ride again? ① ② ③ ④ ⑤

Weather ☀ ☁ ⛅ 🌧 🌨   Temperature

QUOTE OF THE DAY

What the hell of a tour ① ② ③ ④ ⑤

MY TOUR LOG

Name

Date	Location
Time	Bike Park ☐ Trail Park ☐ Cross Country ☐
Total Time	Ø Speed Top Speed
Distance	Elevation Gain

Bike

Riders along

Difficulty ① ② ③ ④ ⑤   Fitness level ① ② ③ ④ ⑤

Fun factor ① ② ③ ④ ⑤   Ride again?   ① ② ③ ④ ⑤

Weather   Temperature

QUOTE OF THE DAY

What the hell of a tour   ① ② ③ ④ ⑤

MY TOUR LOG

Name

Date

Location

Time

Bike Park ☐   Trail Park ☐   Cross Country ☐

Total Time

Ø Speed   Top Speed

Distance   Elevation Gain

Bike

Riders along

Difficulty   ① ② ③ ④ ⑤   Fitness level   ① ② ③ ④ ⑤

Fun factor   ① ② ③ ④ ⑤   Ride again?   ① ② ③ ④ ⑤

Weather ☀ ☁ ⛅ 🌧 🌨   Temperature

QUOTE OF THE DAY

What the hell of a tour   ①   ②   ③   ④   ⑤

MY TOUR LOG

Name

Date

Time

Total Time

Distance

Bike

Riders along

Location

Bike Park ☐ Trail Park ☐ Cross Country ☐

Ø Speed   Top Speed

Elevation Gain

Difficulty	① ② ③ ④ ⑤	Fitness level ① ② ③ ④ ⑤
Fun factor	① ② ③ ④ ⑤	Ride again? ① ② ③ ④ ⑤

Weather ☀ ☁ 🌤 🌧 🌨   Temperature

QUOTE OF THE DAY

What the hell of a tour   ① ② ③ ④ ⑤

MY TOUR LOG

Name

Date | Location

Time | Bike Park ☐ Trail Park ☐ Cross Country ☐

Total Time | Ø Speed | Top Speed

Distance | Elevation Gain

Bike

Riders along

Difficulty ① ② ③ ④ ⑤   Fitness level ① ② ③ ④ ⑤

Fun factor ① ② ③ ④ ⑤   Ride again? ① ② ③ ④ ⑤

Weather ☀ ☁ ⛅ 🌧 🌨   Temperature

QUOTE OF THE DAY

What the hell of a tour ① ② ③ ④ ⑤

MY TOUR LOG

Name

Date

Location

Time

Bike Park ☐   Trail Park ☐   Cross Country ☐

Total Time

Ø Speed

Top Speed

Distance

Elevation Gain

Bike

Riders along

Difficulty   ① ② ③ ④ ⑤   Fitness level   ① ② ③ ④ ⑤

Fun factor   ① ② ③ ④ ⑤   Ride again?   ① ② ③ ④ ⑤

Weather   ☀ ☁ ⛅ 🌧 🌨   Temperature

QUOTE OF THE DAY

What the hell of a tour   **1**   **2**   **3**   **4**   **5**

MY TOUR LOG

Name

Date

Location

Time

Bike Park ☐ Trail Park ☐ Cross Country ☐

Total Time

Ø Speed

Top Speed

Distance

Elevation Gain

Bike

Riders along

Difficulty ① ② ③ ④ ⑤

Fitness level ① ② ③ ④ ⑤

Fun factor ① ② ③ ④ ⑤

Ride again? ① ② ③ ④ ⑤

Weather ☀ ☁ ⛅ 🌧 🌨 Temperature

QUOTE OF THE DAY

What the hell of a tour ① ② ③ ④ ⑤

MY TOUR LOG

Name

Date

Location

Time

Bike Park ☐ Trail Park ☐ Cross Country ☐

Total Time

Ø Speed

Top Speed

Distance

Elevation Gain

Bike

Riders along

Difficulty (1) (2) (3) (4) (5)   Fitness level (1) (2) (3) (4) (5)

Fun factor (1) (2) (3) (4) (5)   Ride again? (1) (2) (3) (4) (5)

Weather ☀ ☁ 🌤 🌧 🌨   Temperature

QUOTE OF THE DAY

What the hell of a tour   (1)   (2)   (3)   (4) (5)

MY TOUR LOG

Name

Date

Time   Bike Park ☐   Trail Park ☐   Cross Country ☐

Total Time   Ø Speed   Top Speed

Distance   Elevation Gain

Bike

Riders along

Difficulty   ① ② ③ ④ ⑤   Fitness level   ① ② ③ ④ ⑤

Fun factor   ① ② ③ ④ ⑤   Ride again?   ① ② ③ ④ ⑤

Weather   ☀   ☁   ⛅   🌧   🌨   Temperature

QUOTE OF THE DAY

What the hell of a tour   ① ② ③ ④ ⑤

MY TOUR LOG

Name

Date

Location

Time

Bike Park ☐   Trail Park ☐   Cross Country ☐

Total Time

Ø Speed   Top Speed

Distance

Elevation Gain

Bike

Riders along

Difficulty	① ② ③ ④ ⑤	Fitness level	① ② ③ ④ ⑤
Fun factor	① ② ③ ④ ⑤	Ride again?	① ② ③ ④ ⑤

Weather   ☀   ☁   ⛅   🌧   🌨   Temperature

QUOTE OF THE DAY

What the hell of a tour

MY TOUR LOG

Name

Date

Location

Time

Bike Park ☐ Trail Park ☐ Cross Country ☐

Total Time

Ø Speed

Top Speed

Distance

Elevation Gain

Bike

Riders along

Difficulty	① ② ③ ④ ⑤	Fitness level	① ② ③ ④ ⑤
Fun factor	① ② ③ ④ ⑤	Ride again?	① ② ③ ④ ⑤

Weather ☀ ☁ ⛅ 🌧 🌨 Temperature

QUOTE OF THE DAY

What the hell of a tour   ④ ⑤

MY TOUR LOG

Name

Date _____ Location _____

Time _____ Bike Park ☐ Trail Park ☐ Cross Country ☐

Total Time _____ Ø Speed _____ Top Speed _____

Distance _____ Elevation Gain _____

Bike _____

Riders along _____

_____

Difficulty ① ② ③ ④ ⑤   Fitness level ① ② ③ ④ ⑤

Fun factor ① ② ③ ④ ⑤   Ride again? ① ② ③ ④ ⑤

Weather ☀ ☁ 🌦 🌧 🌨   Temperature _____

QUOTE OF THE DAY

What the hell of a tour

MY TOUR LOG

Name

Date

Location

Time

Bike Park ☐ Trail Park ☐ Cross Country ☐

Total Time

Ø Speed

Top Speed

Distance

Elevation Gain

Bike

Riders along

Difficulty   ① ② ③ ④ ⑤   Fitness level   ① ② ③ ④ ⑤

Fun factor   ① ② ③ ④ ⑤   Ride again?   ① ② ③ ④ ⑤

Weather ☀ ☁ ⛅ 🌧 🌨   Temperature

QUOTE OF THE DAY

What the hell of a tour   ① ② ③ ④ ⑤

MY TOUR LOG

Name

Date

Time

Total Time

Distance

Bike

Riders along

Location

Bike Park ☐ Trail Park ☐ Cross Country ☐

Ø Speed   Top Speed

Elevation Gain

Difficulty	①	②	③	④	⑤

Difficulty   ① ② ③ ④ ⑤   Fitness level   ① ② ③ ④ ⑤

Fun factor   ① ② ③ ④ ⑤   Ride again?   ① ② ③ ④ ⑤

Weather   ☀ ☁ 🌤 🌧 🌨   Temperature

QUOTE OF THE DAY

What the hell of a tour   ① ② ③ ④ ⑤

MY TOUR LOG

Name

Date	Location
Time	Bike Park ☐ Trail Park ☐ Cross Country ☐
Total Time	Ø Speed Top Speed
Distance	Elevation Gain
Bike	
Riders along	

Difficulty ① ② ③ ④ ⑤   Fitness level ① ② ③ ④ ⑤

Fun factor ① ② ③ ④ ⑤   Ride again? ① ② ③ ④ ⑤

Weather ☀ ☁ 🌤 🌧 🌨   Temperature

QUOTE OF THE DAY

What the hell of a tour ① ② ③ ④ ⑤

MY TOUR LOG

Name

Date | Location

Time | Bike Park ☐ Trail Park ☐ Cross Country ☐

Total Time | Ø Speed | Top Speed

Distance | Elevation Gain

Bike

Riders along

Difficulty   ① ② ③ ④ ⑤   Fitness level   ① ② ③ ④ ⑤

Fun factor   ① ② ③ ④ ⑤   Ride again?   ① ② ③ ④ ⑤

Weather ☀ ⛅ 🌤 🌧 🌨   Temperature

QUOTE OF THE DAY

What the hell of a tour   ① ② ③ ④ ⑤

MY TOUR LOG

Name

Date   Location

Time   Bike Park ☐   Trail Park ☐   Cross Country ☐

Total Time   Ø Speed   Top Speed

Distance   Elevation Gain

Bike

Riders along

Difficulty   ① ② ③ ④ ⑤   Fitness level   ① ② ③ ④ ⑤

Fun factor   ① ② ③ ④ ⑤   Ride again?   ① ② ③ ④ ⑤

Weather   ☀   ☁   🌦   🌧   🌨   Temperature

QUOTE OF THE DAY

What the hell of a tour   ①   ②   ③   ④   ⑤

MY TOUR LOG

Name

Date		Location
Time		Bike Park ☐ Trail Park ☐ Cross Country ☐
Total Time		Ø Speed	Top Speed
Distance		Elevation Gain
Bike	
Riders along	

Difficulty	① ② ③ ④ ⑤	Fitness level	① ② ③ ④ ⑤
Fun factor	① ② ③ ④ ⑤	Ride again?	① ② ③ ④ ⑤

Weather ☀ ☁ 🌦 🌧 🌨 Temperature

QUOTE OF THE DAY

What the hell of a tour   ① ② ③ ④ ⑤

MY TOUR LOG

Name

Date _____ Location _____

Time _____ Bike Park ☐ Trail Park ☐ Cross Country ☐

Total Time _____ Ø Speed _____ Top Speed _____

Distance _____ Elevation Gain _____

Bike _____

Riders along _____

_____

Difficulty ① ② ③ ④ ⑤   Fitness level ① ② ③ ④ ⑤

Fun factor ① ② ③ ④ ⑤   Ride again? ① ② ③ ④ ⑤

Weather ☀ ⛅ 🌤 🌧 🌨   Temperature _____

QUOTE OF THE DAY

What the hell of a tour

MY TOUR LOG

Name

Date

Location

Time

Bike Park ☐ Trail Park ☐ Cross Country ☐

Total Time

Ø Speed

Top Speed

Distance

Elevation Gain

Bike

Riders along

Difficulty ① ② ③ ④ ⑤

Fitness level ① ② ③ ④ ⑤

Fun factor ① ② ③ ④ ⑤

Ride again? ① ② ③ ④ ⑤

Weather ☀ ☁ ⛅ 🌧 🌨 Temperature

QUOTE OF THE DAY

What the hell of a tour ① ② ③ ④ ⑤

MY TOUR LOG

Name

Date _____ Location _____

Time _____ Bike Park ☐ Trail Park ☐ Cross Country ☐

Total Time _____ Ø Speed _____ Top Speed _____

Distance _____ Elevation Gain _____

Bike _____

Riders along _____

_____

Difficulty ① ② ③ ④ ⑤   Fitness level ① ② ③ ④ ⑤

Fun factor ① ② ③ ④ ⑤   Ride again? ① ② ③ ④ ⑤

Weather ☀ ⛅ 🌤 🌧 🌨   Temperature _____

QUOTE OF THE DAY

What the hell of a tour ① ② ③ ④ ⑤

MY TOUR LOG

Name

Date

Location

Time

Bike Park ☐   Trail Park ☐   Cross Country ☐

Total Time

Ø Speed

Top Speed

Distance

Elevation Gain

Bike

Riders along

Difficulty   ① ② ③ ④ ⑤   Fitness level   ① ② ③ ④ ⑤

Fun factor   ① ② ③ ④ ⑤   Ride again?   ① ② ③ ④ ⑤

Weather   ☀️ ⛅ 🌦️ 🌧️ 🌨️   Temperature

QUOTE OF THE DAY

What the hell of a tour   1   2   3   4   5

MY TOUR LOG

Name

Date

Time   Bike Park ☐   Trail Park ☐   Cross Country ☐

Total Time   Ø Speed   Top Speed

Distance   Elevation Gain

Bike

Riders along

Difficulty	① ② ③ ④ ⑤	Fitness level	① ② ③ ④ ⑤
Fun factor	① ② ③ ④ ⑤	Ride again?	① ② ③ ④ ⑤

Weather   ☀   ☁   🌤   🌧   🌨   Temperature

QUOTE OF THE DAY

What the hell of a tour   ①   ②   ③   ④   ⑤

MY TOUR LOG

Name

Date	Location
Time	Bike Park ☐ Trail Park ☐ Cross Country ☐
Total Time	Ø Speed Top Speed
Distance	Elevation Gain

Bike

Riders along

Difficulty	① ② ③ ④ ⑤		Fitness level	① ② ③ ④ ⑤	
Fun factor	① ② ③ ④ ⑤		Ride again?	① ② ③ ④ ⑤	

Weather   Temperature

QUOTE OF THE DAY

What the hell of a tour   ① ② ③ ④ ⑤

MY TOUR LOG

Name

Date		Location	

Time | | Bike Park ☐   Trail Park ☐   Cross Country ☐

Total Time | | Ø Speed | | Top Speed |

Distance | | Elevation Gain |

Bike

Riders along

Difficulty	① ② ③ ④ ⑤	Fitness level	① ② ③ ④ ⑤
Fun factor	① ② ③ ④ ⑤	Ride again?	① ② ③ ④ ⑤

Weather ☀ ☁ ⛅ 🌧 🌨   Temperature ☐

QUOTE OF THE DAY

What the hell of a tour

MY TOUR LOG

Name

Date	Location
Time	Bike Park ☐ Trail Park ☐ Cross Country ☐
Total Time	Ø Speed Top Speed
Distance	Elevation Gain
Bike	
Riders along	

Difficulty ① ② ③ ④ ⑤   Fitness level ① ② ③ ④ ⑤

Fun factor ① ② ③ ④ ⑤   Ride again? ① ② ③ ④ ⑤

Weather ☀ ⛅ 🌤 🌧 🌨   Temperature

QUOTE OF THE DAY

What the hell of a tour   ④ ⑤

MY TOUR LOG

Name

Date | Location

Time | Bike Park ☐ Trail Park ☐ Cross Country ☐

Total Time | Ø Speed | Top Speed

Distance | Elevation Gain

Bike

Riders along

Difficulty ① ② ③ ④ ⑤ | Fitness level ① ② ③ ④ ⑤

Fun factor ① ② ③ ④ ⑤ | Ride again? ① ② ③ ④ ⑤

Weather ☀ ☁ ⛅ 🌧 🌨 Temperature

QUOTE OF THE DAY

What the hell of a tour

MY TOUR LOG

Name

Date

Time

Total Time

Distance

Bike

Riders along

Location

Bike Park ☐   Trail Park ☐   Cross Country ☐

Ø Speed   Top Speed

Elevation Gain

Difficulty	① ② ③ ④ ⑤	Fitness level	① ② ③ ④ ⑤
Fun factor	① ② ③ ④ ⑤	Ride again?	① ② ③ ④ ⑤

Weather ☼ ☁ ⛅ 🌧 🌨   Temperature

QUOTE OF THE DAY

What the hell of a tour   ①   ②   ③   ④   ⑤

MY TOUR LOG

Name

Date _____ Location _____

Time _____ Bike Park ☐ Trail Park ☐ Cross Country ☐

Total Time _____ Ø Speed _____ Top Speed _____

Distance _____ Elevation Gain _____

Bike _____

Riders along _____

_____

Difficulty ① ② ③ ④ ⑤   Fitness level ① ② ③ ④ ⑤

Fun factor ① ② ③ ④ ⑤   Ride again? ① ② ③ ④ ⑤

Weather ☀ ☁ ⛅ 🌧 🌨   Temperature _____

QUOTE OF THE DAY

What the hell of a tour ① ② ③ ④ ⑤

MY TOUR LOG

Name

Date

Location

Time

Bike Park ☐ Trail Park ☐ Cross Country ☐

Total Time

Ø Speed

Top Speed

Distance

Elevation Gain

Bike

Riders along

Difficulty ① ② ③ ④ ⑤

Fitness level ① ② ③ ④ ⑤

Fun factor ① ② ③ ④ ⑤

Ride again? ① ② ③ ④ ⑤

Weather

Temperature

QUOTE OF THE DAY

What the hell of a tour   ④ ⑤

MY TOUR LOG

Name

Date	Location
Time	Bike Park ☐ Trail Park ☐ Cross Country ☐
Total Time	Ø Speed Top Speed
Distance	Elevation Gain

Bike

Riders along

Difficulty ① ② ③ ④ ⑤   Fitness level ① ② ③ ④ ⑤

Fun factor ① ② ③ ④ ⑤   Ride again? ① ② ③ ④ ⑤

Weather ☀ ☁ 🌤 🌧 🌨   Temperature

QUOTE OF THE DAY

What the hell of a tour ① ② ③ ④ ⑤

MY TOUR LOG

Name

Date   Location

Time   Bike Park ☐   Trail Park ☐   Cross Country ☐

Total Time   Ø Speed   Top Speed

Distance   Elevation Gain

Bike

Riders along

Difficulty   ① ② ③ ④ ⑤   Fitness level   ① ② ③ ④ ⑤

Fun factor   ① ② ③ ④ ⑤   Ride again?   ① ② ③ ④ ⑤

Weather   ☀   ☁   ⛅   🌧   🌨   Temperature

QUOTE OF THE DAY

What the hell of a tour   ⑤

MY TOUR LOG

Name

Date		Location	
Time		Bike Park ☐ Trail Park ☐ Cross Country ☐
Total Time		Ø Speed		Top Speed	
Distance		Elevation Gain	
Bike	
Riders along	

Difficulty ① ② ③ ④ ⑤   Fitness level ① ② ③ ④ ⑤

Fun factor ① ② ③ ④ ⑤   Ride again? ① ② ③ ④ ⑤

Weather   Temperature

QUOTE OF THE DAY

What the hell of a tour ① ② ③ ④ ⑤

MY TOUR LOG

Name

Date

Time

Total Time

Distance

Bike

Riders along

Location

Bike Park ☐ Trail Park ☐ Cross Country ☐

Ø Speed   Top Speed

Elevation Gain

Difficulty	① ② ③ ④ ⑤	Fitness level	① ② ③ ④ ⑤
Fun factor	① ② ③ ④ ⑤	Ride again?	① ② ③ ④ ⑤

Weather ☀ ☁ 🌤 🌧 🌨   Temperature

QUOTE OF THE DAY

What the hell of a tour   ④ ⑤

MY TOUR LOG

Name

Date

Location

Time

Bike Park ☐ Trail Park ☐ Cross Country ☐

Total Time

Ø Speed

Top Speed

Distance

Elevation Gain

Bike

Riders along

Difficulty ① ② ③ ④ ⑤

Fitness level ① ② ③ ④ ⑤

Fun factor ① ② ③ ④ ⑤

Ride again? ① ② ③ ④ ⑤

Weather

Temperature

QUOTE OF THE DAY

What the hell of a tour   ④ ⑤

MY TOUR LOG

Name

Date	Location
Time	Bike Park ☐ Trail Park ☐ Cross Country ☐
Total Time	Ø Speed Top Speed
Distance	Elevation Gain

Bike

Riders along

Difficulty	① ② ③ ④ ⑤
Fun factor	① ② ③ ④ ⑤

Fitness level	① ② ③ ④ ⑤
Ride again?	① ② ③ ④ ⑤

Weather ☀ ☁ 🌤 🌧 🌨 Temperature

QUOTE OF THE DAY

What the hell of a tour   ①   ②   ③   ④   ⑤

Contact:

Gerald Curk Marketing & Design
Waldschmidtstraße 9 • 93051 Regensburg
GERMANY

Any questions or suggestions: servus@curk.de

Made in United States
Orlando, FL
13 December 2022

26535474R00062